WONDERFUL WORLD OF—
HORSES
Color & Story Album

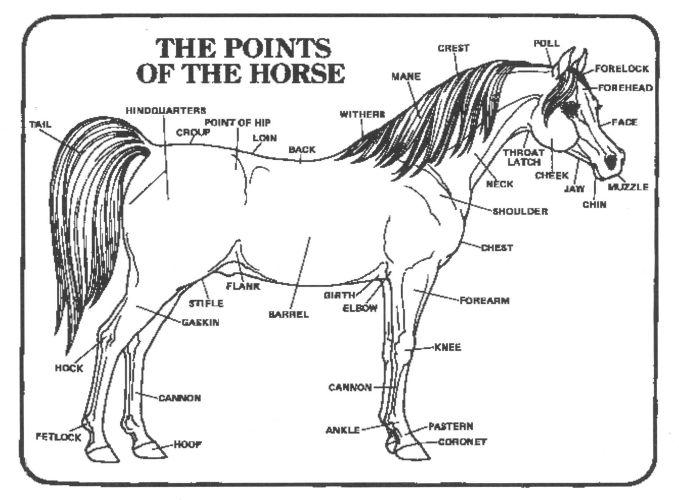

THE POINTS OF THE HORSE

CREST · POLL · FORELOCK · FOREHEAD · MANE · WITHERS · FACE · THROAT LATCH · CHEEK · MUZZLE · JAW · CHIN · NECK · SHOULDER · CHEST · FOREARM · GIRTH · ELBOW · KNEE · CANNON · ANKLE · PASTERN · CORONET

TAIL · HINDQUARTERS · POINT OF HIP · CROUP · LOIN · BACK · FLANK · STIFLE · BARREL · GASKIN · HOCK · CANNON · FETLOCK · HOOF

Written and illustrated by Rita Warner
Cover illustration by Bill Farnsworth
(Formerly *Wonderful World of Horses Coloring Album*)

TROUBADOR PRESS
an imprint of

PRICE STERN SLOAN

ISBN: 0-8431-7415-3

2007 Printing

EOHIPPUS – PLIOHIPPUS – EQUUS – EQUUS CABALLUS

Scientists believe Eohippus to be the first in line of the prehistoric horses — the original ancestor of the modern horse. Even though Eohippus and the modern animal do not resemble each other, their skeletal structures have many things in common. The skeletal and fossil remains of Eohippus can be seen in natural history museums. Eohippus, meaning dawn horse, roamed the plains of North America some fifty million years ago. These were very small creatures, less than a foot in height, with four soft toes on the front feet and three on the back. The only defense they had against enemies was to run away.

All animal species develop in response to their environment, and after millions of years, Eohippus changed so much that the genus became known as Pliohippus. Although Pliohippus was still quite small, he began to resemble the modern horse. The center toe of each foot was very long with a developing thick horny nail, and the side toes had almost disappeared.

From Pliohippus evolved Equus, the first prehistoric horse that was really similar to the modern one. They looked much like the contemporary pony, with a flying mane and tail. During the Ice Ages, Equus became extinct in North America for reasons unknown. Probably because their natural foods disappeared, this horse was forced to migrate to other parts of the world.

Four types of horses developed from Equus in different areas, as a result of various environments. These types provided the foundation for the modern horse, and are as follows:

Equus przewalskii — from the steppes of Central Asia. This horse had great strength and speed. It was reddish or dark brown and small, standing only 48 inches tall at the withers. From the przewalskii were derived the Japanese, Mongolian and Korean ponies.

Equus tarpannus — from the cold barren wastelands and rocky, mountainous regions of Russia. Dun in color, this horse was the source of the ponies and other horses ridden in Asian invasions. It spread to Norway and Britain and became the Celtic horse found there several centuries ago.

Equus robustus — lived in Europe where climates were mild and food was plentiful. This cold-blooded type was very large and easily domesticated. It looked much like the draft horse of today which apparently evolved from the robustus. The term cold-blooded is still used to refer to horses that have a draft breed in their ancestry.

Equus agilis — the hot-blooded horse of the dry plains and deserts of Africa and Arabia. Hot-blooded alludes to the Eastern ancestry of a horse, and is used to denote a high-spirited temperament. From this slender, swift-moving animal developed the Arabian and Barb strains and all other horses known as the light breeds. This term still refers to any horse not of draft lineage.

The modern horse is called Equus caballus, and is much faster than its ancestors. The body has become larger and stronger, with the eyes positioned so that danger can be seen in all directions. Just like the first prehistoric horses, Equus caballus always stays on the alert and ready to run.

A horse's height is measured in hands, and each hand equals four inches. Thus, 14:3 means the horse stands 14 hands plus 3 inches high, or a total of 59 inches from withers to ground. The life-span of this animal is approximately 30 years, although some breeds live longer. At birth all horses are called foals, although filly refers to a female, and colt to a male foal. Regardless of which month a foal is born, on January 1 of the following year it is considered a year old, or a yearling. A horse has fully developed in 5 years, with some breeds maturing earlier or later than others. Adult female horses are called mares and male horses are stallions. When they become parents, the mother is known as a dam, and the father as a sire.

No one really knows just how long ago man first tamed the horse — perhaps as far back as 3500 B.C. Man's principal use of horses has always been for work. Down through the centuries, horses played an important part in war, agriculture and transportation. Through selective breeding, various breeds have been developed for very specific purposes — some for the show-ring, utility, or for pleasure. There is an old quotation which goes: ''There is something about the outside of a horse that is good for the inside of a man.'' This fascination and love of horses will live on in the minds and hearts of the human race for many more centuries to come.

THE ARABIAN

The Arabian is the oldest and purest breed of horse in the world. The origin of these horses is a mystery to historians. It is known, however, that hot-blooded horses evolved on the high open plains and dry deserts of Northern Africa, Arabia, and surrounding regions. The severe existence in these arid climates caused the desert horses to develop trim muscular bodies with sleek coats, black skin to resist sunburn, slender sturdy legs free of long hair, hard bones, small sound feet for fleetness, large hearts for endurance, great resistance to disease, alertness, high spirits, courage and intelligence. In all respects, Arabians have inherited these characteristics, plus exceptionally attractive looks.

The outstanding qualities of these desert horses were developed further by Bedouin nomads of the Arabian deserts many centuries ago. Their horses had to be able to take extreme temperature changes and to exist on sparse amounts of food and water. The feet and legs had to withstand fast galloping over terrain that shifted from deep soft sand to stony earth. Although these people led a primitive existence, they managed to skillfully master the first recorded selective breeding of horses. Their breeding program was very strict and pedigrees were kept carefully.

Today the Arabian's gentle disposition traces to the ways in which the Bedouins treated their horses — as companions and pets, with much love and devotion. Arabian horses all over the world are still bred with the same loyalty that goes back more than a thousand years.

There is no official registry for Arabians in their native country. Families there still keep accurate records of breeding, with some going back as far as 300 years. Before 1908, when the first Arabian horse registry was formed in the United States, there were very few *pure* horses of this strain in the country.

Even though Arabians came from the desert, they easily adapt to all climates and conditions. Through long association with people, they have developed a degree of understanding not usually found in other breeds. Arabian horses are very affectionate and react more readily to human commands.

Originally small horses, Arabians of today stand from 14:1 to 15:2 hands. They display long silky manes and tails, and coats of a smooth satin finish. Their coloring is more vivid than most breeds, coming in brilliant chestnut, liver-chestnut, flashy bay, chocolate-brown, steel-gray, rose-gray, snowy white and jet-black. White markings, such as a blaze or star on the face and white stockings on the legs, are common, especially in the chestnuts, bays and browns. Unless crossed with other breeds, Arabians are never spotted.

With their magnificent spirit, and stylish and low springy action, Arabians make delightful saddle horses. Their walk is even and smooth, their natural slightly choppy trot can be easily refined. Their canter seems like a rocking chair and they have a swift gallop.

Arabians are highly regarded as show horses and appear in classes at halter, under saddle — both English and Western type — and in harness. They are excellent jumpers, and valuable ranch horses. Their great stamina makes them one of the most preferred trail horses.

The only horse breed whose features today are the same as those of their ancient ancestors, is the Arabian. They have been so potent in transmitting their fixed characteristics that all light horse breeds have been influenced by the blood of these horses.

With an elegance all their own, they carry the neck proudly in a classic arch and the tail flung high. Their striking and beautifully sculptured head shows off a dished or slightly concave face, large and lustrous dark eyes set wide, neat little ears tipped inward, and a small tapered muzzle with flared nostrils. The handsome Arabian is perhaps the most admired of all horses.

THE THOROUGHBRED

Horse racing, the "sport of kings", belongs to the Thoroughbred, who is carefully bred and trained to race. Hundreds of years ago, this sport was for the exclusive amusement of gentry and noblemen in England. Only they could afford to breed horses especially for speed.

The Thoroughbred was created in England, beginning in the seventeenth and eighteenth centuries, when hot-blooded desert-bred stallions were imported to improve the racing stock. Early English breeders found that the fleet desert horse, when crossed with their native mares, produced an animal with greater speed, good height and length, sturdiness and a longer stride.

The most prominent foundation sires of the Thoroughbred breed were the Byerly Turk, brought to England in 1689; the Darley Arabian who arrived in 1706; and the Godolphin Barb, imported in 1724. All Thoroughbreds today, and many other breeds, can be traced back to these three great sires.

Thoroughbreds clearly display quality and refinement in their long and muscular frame. The handsome and excellent head, with full bright eyes, sits gracefully on a long slender neck. The chest is narrow, deep and well-developed, and the muscular shoulders are set at an angle. The back is short and strong, with powerful hindquarters for propulsion. Good bone supports long clean legs, and the pasterns act as shock absorbers. The withers of this lean animal are peaked and higher than the croup, and the mane and tail grow in thin and fine.

Rough treatment of the Thoroughbred results in a spoiled horse, because of their sensitive and easily excitable nature. They require a great deal of firm, but gentle handling. They are high-spirited, timid and delicate, yet willing, courageous and durable. For everyday hacking — riding — these highly-bred, intelligent animals delight experienced riders.

Thoroughbreds make excellent show-jumpers, steeplechasers and dressage performers. Their blood is often crossed with other breeds to produce good polo ponies and hunters.

Modern Thoroughbreds stand much taller than their ancestors, with heights ranging from 15 to 17 hands. Their colors are commonly brown, bay, black or chestnut and sometimes roan or gray. Some have white markings on the face and legs.

The name Thoroughbred should not be confused with purebred — all other breeds of horses are purebred. Thoroughbred applies to only one particular breed of horse.

The racing of registered Thoroughbreds in America began in 1745 at Annapolis, Maryland. In 1788, the famed Messenger was imported. He is considered the greatest sire of runners, and also of trotters. His grandson, Hambletonian, founded the Standardbred trotters and pacers. Messenger is also the grandsire of Eclipse, who was never beaten.

The most celebrated Thoroughbred in American racing history was Man O' War. He won every race he entered except one — there he was beaten by a horse named Upset. Man O' War became so famous that a statue was erected over his grave.

The best known and most popular horse race in America is the Kentucky Derby. It admits only three-year-old Thoroughbreds, and has been run since 1875 at Churchill Downs in Louisville, Kentucky. The middle Southern states, including Kentucky, are real Thoroughbred country, where the conditions are the most suitable for producing the best horses.

Today Thoroughbred racing means big business. Horses who have proved their worth on the track sell for thousands of dollars. Each year new records of speed are made and the value of these horses keeps rising.

Thoroughbreds have the stamina to race a mile — 1,760 yards — or further. They have a large heart and lungs for great wind. At top speed they can run 40 miles per hour while carrying a jockey, weighing 125 pounds or more, in his colorful racing silks. No other breed can stay with Thoroughbreds at this distance on the track, for these horses have an unending determination to win.

THE MUSTANG

Many parts of America would probably still be wilderness if it were not for the small but hardy wild horses, the Mustangs. These horses roamed in large numbers over the plains and mountains of the West several hundred years ago. With its huge expanses of untamed country, this land provided a refuge and life of freedom for the Mustangs. They were free from men on their backs, sharp spurs, heavy saddles and painful bits. They drank from cool streams and grazed on the rich grass of the prairies. Their shelter was in hidden forests and the folds of canyon walls.

The Mustang's name comes from the Spanish word *mesteno,* which means unclaimed. They are descended from the horses of Arabian and Barb ancestry who were brought to Mexico and the United States by Spanish conquistadors and explorers, beginning around fifteen-hundred. These hot-blooded horses possessed great stamina. They had strong bones and were full of fire. The ones that survived battles and death from natural causes multiplied and began to run in small bands. The offspring of these horses, later to become known as Mustangs, scattered throughout Mexico, the Southwestern states and as far as the Pacific Northwest. These were the first horses in North America since Equus, the horse of the Ice Age.

The wild little Mustangs became tougher, swifter and wiser. Each band was headed by a powerful stallion, who guarded them from intruders and predators. He would stand like a statue on high ground or a mountain ledge. He would fight to protect his mares, their foals and the yearlings — even dying for them.

Averaging 14:2 hands, Mustangs came in many colors: black, silver-grey, white, brown, sorrel, bay, blue or red roan, dun and cream. Their colors blended with the countryside and certain hues dominated in different parts of the land. They were usually solidly colored, but with later mutations there appeared calico horses called pintos, meaning to paint. The pinto was good camouflage against the rocks and brush of mountain, desert and prairie. There are two types of pinto: the piebald whose colors are black and white, and the skewbald whose colors are white and any color other than black. When the white spreads up from the belly, a pinto is classified as an overo — when it spreads down from the back, this horse is known as a tobiano.

The Indians, who had never seen a horse before the arrival of the conquistadors, captured, gentled and broke many of the Mustangs. They became excellent horsemen and rode bareback without bridles, needing the use of their hands for holding weapons. Indians preferred to ride the unusually colorful pintos to battle because their white patches made a good background for warpaint.

With the coming of the settlers to the Western frontier, the Mustang's freedom dwindled. These people, like the Indians, caught and broke the horses to ride, pull wagons and plow fields.

Mustangs lacked fine breeding, beauty and flash, but they made up for it in spirit, stamina and courage. Their blood was infused with other strains including the Quarter Horse, Morgan and Thoroughbred, which produced durable and reliable cowponies and remounts for the cavalry and Pony Express. Some Mustangs were even used in rodeos as bucking broncos, for although they were captured, they were still outlaws — so savage that few men could gentle them.

The wild horses running in some of the Western states today should not be mistaken for Mustangs. These horses, who probably broke free from ranchers' herds, are a mixture of breeds with only a trace of Spanish blood. They are rangy and their qualities have greatly diminished. These are the wild horses who have been hunted down by man over the past few decades for meat. But in 1971, Congress passed a law giving them national sanctuary against hunters.

There are few *genuine* Mustangs left. No more can they be found on the open rangeland — they don't canter over hilltops or tiptoe up rocky mountain ledges. The little *mesteno* — the runaway horse — lives only in history as a symbol of the Old West.

THE APPALOOSA

The Appaloosa is an ancient breed whose unusually marked coats have been discovered in the wall drawings of European Ice Age caves, and found in Chinese works of art dating back to 500 B.C. According to Greek records, Persians rode spotted war horses. Legendary writings reveal that these horses were regarded as sacred.

Although the Appaloosa breed has a long history, the name is relatively new. Inhabiting parts of Northwestern United States a couple of centuries ago, was an Indian tribe known as the Nez Perce. They had beautiful horses with coats of various patterns and colors. No one knows how or when these Indians acquired their horses. Perhaps they descended from the spotted strains among those horses brought to the New World by Spaniards in the sixteenth century. These animals must have appealed greatly to the Nez Perce for they were considered one of the most colorful tribes. The artistic beaded designs in their clothing and horse trappings were outstanding.

The Appaloosa was first known as the Palousy. This name was taken from a small stream, the Palouse, which flows through the Grand Ronde Valley and into the mighty Snake River in Southeast Washington. This valley was the home of the Nez Perce Indians and its lush fertile floor, surrounded by immense mountains, made a perfect breeding ground for horses.

One Nez Perce leader, the great Chief Joseph, was among the most noted horse breeders of his time. The tribe practiced what is called selective breeding. By sorting out and trading away the inferior animals, they kept and bred only the best mares to the best stallions. Over many years, Appaloosas became some of the most distinctive and highly bred horses in America.

The Nez Perce created what they referred to as their "buffalo horse." In order to hunt and outrun such large tough beasts in that rough country, the Appaloosas had to be hardy, swift and extremely sure-footed. They had to be gentle, dependable mounts because the Indians rode bareback. The warriors needed both hands to use weapons, and controlled their horses by only the means of a thin rawhide rein tied loosely around the horse's lower jaw.

By 1877 the Nez Perce had bred and raised thousands of Appaloosas, but that same year the tribe was almost wiped out in battles with the United States Army. Their prized horses were nearly exterminated by the troops on written orders of the Government. Later, however, interested and concerned horse enthusiasts made drastic moves to save the Appaloosa from extinction. The breed has greatly increased in number and today it is one of the most desired of all horses, popular throughout the world.

Unlike their less showy ancestors who were usually found in black and white, reddish-gray or bluish-gray, today's Appaloosa has characteristic coat markings of several patterns and colors, which can be very pronounced. The main body colors are black, brown, bay, sorrel, chestnut, gray, dun, red-roan or blue-roan with a white "blanket" over the hindquarters on which spots of the same shade as the base coat are spattered. The horses may also appear in white with black, sorrel, chestnut or bay spots of various sizes and shapes over the entire body, or they may be mottled light and dark all over. These markings can also vary and combine to produce numerous other patterns.

To be registered, horses must meet rigid conformation standards besides possessing the Appaloosa coloring. They must have certain traits such as white sclera around the eyes and mottled skin, pink under the white hair and black beneath the dark part of the coat.

Appaloosas have sparse manes and tails, some so scant of hair they are rat-tailed. Many of the breed have hooves marked with vertical black and white stripes.

Averaging 14:2 to 15:3 hands, Appaloosas are compactly built, clean-limbed and well-muscled. They have a gentle disposition, a big heart, good wind and great endurance. These qualities have produced a versatile and rugged ranch, trail and pleasure horse. Appaloosas are seen in parades, rodeos and horse shows. These same qualities created the buffalo horse of so long ago — the dearest possession of the Nez Perce Indians.

THE QUARTER HORSE

In America, the first race horse was the Quarter Horse, also recognized as the country's oldest breed. However, the registry for the Quarter Horse was not established until 1941. For nearly 300 years, this horse had been recognized as a distinct "type" with the breed and name both originating in Colonial Virginia and the Carolinas in the sixteen-hundreds. In these colonies, the English settlers would engage in their favorite pastime of matching two horses in short-distance races which were held on village streets or country paths. The horses who ran these races were required to make fast explosive starts and to maintain full speed for a distance of 440 yards. The races therefore became known as quarter milers. In order to have the thrust for sudden takeoffs, these horses had to be solidly built with powerful hindquarters.

The first quarter-mile running horses were primarily of Spanish origin. Much of the stock brought to the East coast of America and acquired by the settlers was of Spanish blood. The Cherokee, Chickasaw and Choctaw Indians came into possession of Spanish horses from the Southwest and from Spanish settlements in Florida and Georgia. The small horses developed by these Indians were described as having heavy muscles and quick action. When they were crossed with the hardy mounts of the colonists, the early Quarter Horses resulted.

The Quarter Horse breed has founding families rather than a founding sire. However, in 1755 an English Thoroughbred named Janus, a grandson of the Godolphin Barb, was brought to Virginia. Janus contributed a great deal to the fleetness of the Quarter Horse. Although he competed in long-distance races with other Thoroughbreds in England, descriptions by men who had seen him were those of a Quarter Horse. His descendants, generation after generation, were marked with his amazing speed, durability and sturdy physique. More than half of the founding families can be traced back to Janus.

The dominant Quarter Horse families, numbering fourteen, emerged 150 years after the time of Janus. Many were established in Texas, others in Oklahoma, Colorado, Pennsylvania, Ohio, Illinois and Missouri.

Quarter-mile races were being run in the American colonies nearly 200 years before the English Thoroughbred became a recognized breed. But, when English imports and long-distance racing became more popular then the short-distance runs, the Quarter Horse moved West with the frontiersmen. The rugged cattle country became their new home and they quickly developed into intelligent and capable cowponies.

With the coming of the automobile and mechanized farming, many breeds decreased in number. But Quarter Horses, with their inborn cow-sense and abilities as all-around ranch horses, remained in demand.

No other breed can equal the agility this horse has in starting, turning, pivoting, stopping and holding. The rodeo cowboy and girl — the calf roper, steer wrestler, and barrel racer — rely on horses with this talent, especially when there are big prizes at stake.

The height of the Quarter Horse varies from 14:2 to 15:2 hands. The recognized colors of their registry are: bay, brown, black, sorrel, chestnut, dun, red dun, buckskin, palomino, gray, blue roan and red roan. Pintos, Appaloosas, albinos or those with white markings on their bellies are considered ineligible for registration.

The Quarter Horse conformation is stocky and compact, with good sloping shoulders, a closely coupled back, sturdy legs with short cannons, a thick neck set squarely on a deep wide chest, and hindquarters layered with muscle. Their head appears broad and short with dark intelligent eyes and small ears. They are extremely well-balanced and sure-footed, with an easy riding gait.

Quarter Horses are noted for their gentle and docile disposition, their willingness for hard fast work, adaptability, and their lightning speed.

Besides serving as working ranch horses, the preferred mounts of rodeo contestants, popular pleasure horses, skillful polo ponies and show horses, Quarter Horses continue to be used — and remain unbeaten — in quarter-mile racing.

THE MORGAN

The Morgan is one of America's oldest breeds, with the strain beginning in Randolph, Vermont around 1790 when a singing school teacher by the name of Justin Morgan acquired a small sturdy colt in payment of a debt. This colt, who was foaled in 1789, eventually came to be known by the singing master's name.

Justin Morgan, the horse, stood only 14 hands high — small by today's standards. He was a good-looking dark bay with black legs, mane and tail. His fine and tapering head had prominent eyes and small pointed ears. His shoulders were tremendous. His thick crested neck was set well into a wide chest. He had a short back and legs, powerful hindquarters and bulging muscles.

Justin Morgan was used essentially as an all-purpose horse, and with willingness and spirit he served his masters — he had several — in plowing fields, pulling stumps and dragging logs out of the Vermont timberland. He was considered a fine saddle and harness horse and he earned money for his owners from stud fees, racing, and pulling matches. His amazing stamina and strength were tested throughout his lifetime, and according to legend, not only could he outtrot and outrun all of his competitors, but he also won log-pulling contests from far bigger horses.

The outstanding physical characteristics and versatility of Justin Morgan, plus his gentle and docile disposition, made him a remarkable little horse. His own strong traits were consistently passed on to his offspring, regardless of the type of mare with whom he was mated. By the time he died in 1821 at the age of 32, Justin Morgan had established a definite strain, and he is the only founding sire to have a breed named for him.

Not only did he lay the foundation for the Morgan breed, but he contributed greatly to the American Saddle Bred and the Tennessee Walking Horse. His trotting abilities also played an important role in the formation of the Standardbred.

Little is known of Justin Morgan's ancestry, but due to the fineness of his head, his short back and legs and his lasting stamina, horse experts believe he had a strong influx of Arab blood.

The earlier Morgans were used generally for farm work and as fine harness or carriage horses. Their popularity decreased with the coming of the automobile and mechanized farming. After an outstanding record with the Union Cavalry from 1861-1865, a large farm near Middlebury, Vermont, was given to the United States Government about 1900 to be used for improving livestock and for preserving the Morgan breed. Stock was selected at this farm by cavalry officers for remount purposes. The Morgan's conformation, soundness, endurance and good disposition made them one of the most popular mounts for regiments of the United States Cavalry. Today the University of Vermont heads the Morgan Horse Farm, and a large statue of the famous founding sire stands there.

The renewed popularity of the Morgan has spread to all parts of the United States, Mexico, South America and Europe. They make excellent pleasure and show horses under saddle or in harness, and they are popular as trail horses and cowponies on large ranches. Morgans are also preferred by many mounted police to help patrol busy streets and city parks.

Morgans of today are taller and more finely built than their founder, averaging 14:1 to 15:2 hands. The crest of their neck rises higher than other breeds and their manes are full and flowing. Their heavy tail is well-set, long and wavy. They commonly appear in bay, black, brown or chestnut with a few white markings.

Their probable Arab ancestry shows in the high degree of intelligence and elegant carriage. A quick smooth-stepping gait gives them the appearance of floating.

Several types of Morgans have been developed over the past century but they continue to retain the marked physical characteristics, the ruggedness and even temperament passed down through so many generations by Justin Morgan, the "big little horse."

1921
GIVEN BY
THE MORGAN HORSE CLUB
TO THE
U·S·DEPARTMENT OF AGRICULTURE
IN MEMORY OF
JUSTIN MORGAN
WHO DIED IN
1821

THE STANDARDBRED

The Standardbred was developed from trotting and pacing horses of early Colonial America. This horse, a close cousin of the Thoroughbred, is used principally in the sport of light harness racing. In this sport the Standardbred either trots or paces while pulling a driver in a light two-wheeled vehicle called a sulky.

The roots of light harness racing go back to the strict and religious Puritan forefathers who colonized New England. They believed horse racing was a sinful sport. Their definition of racing meant running horses at a full gallop to see which could go the fastest. Trotting, however, was not as fast as a horse could go and could hardly be considered a sinful gait. Since buggies, carriages and roadsters were a part of most households, many private contests took place with horses hitched to these vehicles. Often a farmer challenged his neighbor on country roads and village streets at the trotting speed. These early trotting races were known as brushes. Some were under saddle but usually they were driving matches.

Racing at the trotting speed grew as a sport and spread throughout the country. Two-wheeled vehicles, much heavier than the sulkies now used, replaced the farmers' awkward buggies. The harnesses which hitched the horses to these vehicles were made lighter to permit more speed. Tracks were built especially for trotting races and the sport's speed increased when ball-bearing bicycle wheels were adapted to the sulkies.

Although horseowners had been racing their trotting horses since Colonial times, the Standardbred was not made an official breed until the eighteen-seventies.

Harness races are divided into two types — those for trotters and those for pacers. The Standardbred can develop into either a trotter or a pacer. Some pacers have to be trained to their gait by the use of a leg harness, known as hobbles, which prevents them from trotting. Natural pacers, who do not need to be trained, are called free-legged or clean-gaited pacers.

Trotters move their legs in diagonal pairs — the right front and left rear legs go forward at the same time and then the left front and right rear legs. In this gait the back hoof is placed well in advance of the front hoof and to avoid cutting themselves, most racing trotters spread their back legs to bypass the front feet. The trot of the Standardbred does not resemble the trot of any other horse and is extremely fast.

Pacers move both legs on the same side together — their right legs move forward and then their left legs. The pacing gait is a little faster than the trotting gait.

The Standardbred was named for a "standard" of speed. The standard for one mile trotting is 2 minutes, 30 seconds or better, and for pacing is at least 2 minutes, 25 seconds. Although registration in the United States Trotting Association is based largely on proof of bloodlines, these standard trotting and pacing speeds must be achieved before a Standardbred can be registered in the association.

One of the founding sires of modern harness racers was the English Thoroughbred, Messenger. Not until 1849, however, was the greatest sire in trotting and pacing history born. He was named Hambletonian, a great-grandson of Messenger. Today almost all Standardbreds on the track can be traced directly to him.

Justin Morgan, the founding sire of another American breed, the Morgan horse, contributed much to the Standardbred. The strains of Morgan and Hambletonian were closely intermingled in one of the greatest harness racers of all time — the free-legged pacing stallion, Dan Patch. He was the first of the Standardbreds to clock a mile in less than 2 minutes. He set his official record of 1:55.25 in 1905.

The height of a Standardbred ranges from 14 to 16:2 hands, and they are most commonly colored brown, black, bay or chestnut, and occasionally gray, roan or dun. They are sturdier and heavier for their height than Thoroughbreds. The breed has exceptional durability, energy and an even temperament. Their strong hind legs and hindquarters are set well back, which gives them the power for fast trotting and pacing. Because of their long-striding gait, Standardbreds are seldom used as riding horses. Pacers are particularly uncomfortable to ride with the rough jerking motion of their gait.

The graceful-looking movements of the Standardbred, who steps along so swiftly at a controlled gait, is achieved through selective and careful breeding and many hours of patient and skillful training. Light harness racing is one of the world's most beautiful sports to watch.

THE AMERICAN SADDLE BRED

In American pioneer days, good saddle horses were a necessity, for often the roads were so obstructed with mud holes and bogs that only men on horseback were able to pass through. Also, the colonies — especially in the South — contained immense stretches of cotton, cane and tobacco fields. The Southern plantation owners needed horses with gaits as comfortable as possible. The horses were also required to maintain these gaits for the many hours that their riders spent in the saddle supervising their estates. Horses who possessed pacing and ambling gaits had been used for many years before beauty and conformation were considered. But the wealthy Southern planters were aristocrats who admired beautiful and spirited horses. To meet the needs and desires of these men, a distinct breed was developed with a lofty carriage, lots of style, and easy riding gaits. This new breed became known as the American Saddle Bred. Kentucky, Tennessee, Virginia and West Virginia were the first states to breed this horse.

Although the American Saddle Bred had several stallions as a foundation, one was selected later by the registry's association as the sole founding sire. This was a Thoroughbred named Denmark, who was foaled in Kentucky in 1839. Denmark had the greatest number of registered descendants, and these contributed a great deal to the breed. Saddle Breds are predominantly of Thoroughbred ancestry with introductions of Morgan, Standardbred and other strains.

Saddlers, as they are sometimes called, have been developed into two distinct types: the five-gaited and the three-gaited. The five-gaited Saddlers were derived from the original stock after other modes of transportation became available, and ordinary saddle horses were no longer in demand. These beautifully animated and theatrical horses are known as the "peacocks of the show ring." Five-gaited Saddlers are shown at their three natural gaits of walk, trot and canter, and at two other gaits which must be taught: the rack and the slow gait. The rack, a four-beat high-stepping gait, is extremely fast and flashy with lots of knee action. Each hoof strikes the ground at separate and regular intervals. The horses' backs hardly move at all, and though this gait is comfortable for the rider, it is very distressing to the horse. The slow-gait, also called the stepping pace, is a slow-motion version of the high-speed rack. The legs move in the same four-beat sequence, but the hooves strike the ground at irregular intervals producing an offbeat rhythmic amble. Five-gaited Saddlers are also shown in classes in which they are first ridden under saddle, then unsaddled, hitched to sulkies and driven in harness. These horses are known as combination horses. The five-gaited horses must have great eye appeal and display long flowing manes and tails. Dark colors are preferred, such as bay, dark chestnut, seal brown and blue-black. Gray is not uncommon but large areas of white markings are undesirable.

The three-gaited Saddlers must meet the same requirements in the show-ring as the five-gaited, except that they perform only at the three natural gaits. Also, their manes are clipped off entirely and their tails are plucked or shaved at the top. This type is also known as the Working Saddler, and their pleasing disposition and good manners make them ideal pleasure horses outside the show-ring for all riders. The highly finished five-gaited Saddlers, however, require handling by very experienced equestrians.

American Saddle Breds average from 14:3 to 16:1 hands in height. Their necks are long and gracefully carried in a high arch. They have fine delicate heads with large prominant eyes, and their ears stand alert and are set well forward. Their chests are fairly wide with shoulders deep and sloping. They possess high and defined withers, a short back and heavily muscled hindquarters. One of their greatest attributes is a set of strong clean-cut legs with healthy sound feet. Above all they must be exceptionally sure-footed.

Saddle Breds make very serviceable trail horses, and they are favorites with mounted police. Because of their great endurance and smooth gaits, ranchers use these horses on long cattle drives. The elegant and energetic five-gaited Saddlers are often seen in parades under silver saddlery, and at horse shows in parade horse classes.

Exceptional intelligence is combined with poise, dignity and refined beauty to make the American Saddle Bred a very proud breed.

THE TENNESSEE WALKING HORSE

Over one hundred years ago, in the Middle Basin of Tennessee, a unique breed was created — the Tennessee Walking Horse. The early settlers of this region, who came from Virginia, the Carolinas and other surrounding states, brought with them fine Saddle Breds, Standardbreds, Morgans, Thoroughbreds, Canadian and Narrangansett Pacers. By combining the traits of these great horse families, the foundation was laid for the Tennessee Walker who developed distinctive qualities of its own.

The most prominent characteristic of Tennessee Walkers is their swift and smooth "running walk." This gait is inherited and cannot be taught to a horse who does not possess it naturally. It is a square four-beat gait with a gliding motion, and a bobbing of the head and swinging of the ears accompany each step. Some Walkers are even known to snap their teeth in time. When performing the running walk, these horses will overstride, placing the back hoof ahead of their forehoof print. Traveling at speeds from 6 to 8 miles per hour, Walkers can sustain this gait for long distances without fatigue to themselves or their passengers.

Tennessee Walkers are also known for two other unusual gaits, which have to be taught to them. They are the "flat-foot walk" which is a slow, bold, and even gait; and the "canter" which is a refined gallop with a slow and high rolling motion. The canter is full of spring, rhythm and grace, and is often referred to as the "rocking chair" gait. All three gaits of the Tennessee Walker are extremely easy on the rider.

Tennessee Walking Horses were developed for the purposes of riding, driving, and light farm work. They also became very popular with Southern plantation owners who called them Plantation Walkers. These men needed horses with comfortable gaits that could carry them the many miles necessary for inspecting immense fields. The Tennessee Walker's gaits were favored by country doctors who spent many hours on horseback. The traveling preachers, who rode from church to church practicing their sermons on the way, preferred these fast and steady-walking horses.

The stallion who was chosen as the foundation sire of the Tennessee Walking Horse — when the registry was formed in 1935 — was Allan. This black stallion's ancestry was a mixture of Morgan and Hambletonian, who was the founding sire of the Standardbred. Allan was considered the greatest contributor to the Walking Horse breed.

In Tennessee the water flows over limestone rocks and the soil is rich in minerals, yielding lush nutritious bluegrass. This in turn produced the hardy Tennessee Walkers, making them sound and free from disease. These qualities have been transmitted throughout the breed wherever it is found today.

Typical Walkers are affectionate, gentle and intelligent animals. The breed is seen in a variety of colors including brown, black, bay, chestnut, roan, palomino, white or gray. Their face, legs and body may also be marked with white. Averaging 15:2 hands, they have a long graceful neck, short back, well-built hindquarters, sloping shoulders, slender but strong legs, and sound feet. The Tennessee Walker's head is handsome and refined with bright eyes, prominent nostrils, and pointed well-shaped ears. Their manes and tails are usually left long and flowing.

Each year, on the first Saturday night in September, the best Walking Horses are matched for the title "The Grand Champion Walking Horse of the World." This week-long show — The Tennessee Walking Horse National Celebration — is held in Shelbyville, Tennessee. It began back in 1939 and is the largest Walking Horse show in the world.

The Walker is a popular pleasure, trail and show horse throughout the country. Their good manners and remarkably comfortable gaits make them ideal mounts for novice, middle-aged and elderly riders. For quiet relaxed excursions, the beautiful, poised and dignified Tennessee Walking Horses are indeed a pleasure to ride.

THE HUNTER

Hunting foxes and following hounds on horseback began many centuries ago. In medieval Europe, noblemen hunted this way to destroy the foxes and wolves that devoured game birds and poultry. They also hunted wild boar, deer and other animals in the same manner for food.

As time passed, it was the chasing of the fox cross-country with horses and hounds that increased in popularity. The hunt evolved into a sport for the upper class members of European society.

The British Isles are regarded as the home of the fox-hunting sport, and it was the English who introduced it into the American colonies. It blossomed in Virginia, Maryland, Pennsylvania and the Carolinas, beginning in the middle seventeen-hundreds.

A hunt is a grueling and strenuous sport. It takes a special kind of horse to master such tests as leaping the natural obstacles — fences, stone walls, fallen logs and streams — and galloping headlong uphill and down. The hunter, therefore, must possess size, ruggedness and endurance.

Good hunters are reliable and comfortable to ride with strong lengthy strides. Their shoulders are well-sloped. Their neck is long, powerful and set on a large chest. Their forearms and legs, especially the cannons, have excessive strength to carry the weight, while the hindquarters are deep and muscular for lift over jumps. Hunters must be intelligent and easy to control, with great courage and stamina in order to endure a long day of hard riding.

These horses have to be trained to jump whenever and wherever their riders wish. It takes nearly three years of careful patient work to school hunters before they are ever taken out into the hunt field. If their riders handle them properly, the horses will be useful and competent mounts for many years.

Often standing as tall as 17 hands, hunters are of mixed breeding. Generally, they are part Thoroughbred, crossed with selected large breeds. They are not recognized as a breed, but have developed characteristics that are distinctive from all other horses.

Hunters make very suitable bridle path and trail horses. Some hunters are a top attraction in horse shows but are rarely used on real hunts. Most of these lack the good sense and the durability for a day in the field.

Fox hunting is still quite popular in certain areas of the country. Each hunt club has its own livery or uniform. The men often wear a bright scarlet coat, and a vest of white, buff, yellow or the hunt club colors, with gilt or brass buttons. Their breeches are usually white or buff, and their black boots are topped with brown or club colors. Ladies wear black or grey coats with a collar of the hunt club colors, buff or black breeches, and black boots. All members' hats are usually black velvet with a hard lining.

The hunt staff includes the Master of Foxhounds or commander-in-chief whose responsibility it is to head the hunt, the staff and the field members; the huntsman who is obliged to govern his hounds, his whips, and the field members, and to plan and work the day's hunt; the whippers-in who assist the huntsman and keep track of the hounds, whipping the strays back into the pack; and the field master, who is in charge of the field members or followers of the hunt. Either the Master of Foxhounds or the huntsman carries the hunting horn which is used to signal the hounds and field members.

When the huntsman cries "Hark," it means that a dog has picked up the scent of the fox. A series of short notes on the horn bid the rest of the pack to follow. If the fox is spotted, "Tally-ho" is cheered and the pack runs crying after it. This is succeeded by "gone away-away-away-away," which lets the followers know the hounds have located the fox and off they go at a full gallop.

This is the life of the hunter, an extraordinary horse who well deserves a bucket of oats, a cozy stall and warm blankets after an exhausting day of the chase.

THE PALOMINO

Golden-coated horses with creamy-white manes and tails are found in very old European and Chinese paintings, and there are many tales about the origin of these beautiful animals and how they came to the New World. Some believe that Queen Isabella of Spain had a stable of fine golden horses and presented one of her stallions to a conquistador by the name of Juan del Palomino. It is said that Juan took his horse to Mexico during Spain's conquest, and afterwards stayed on and bred the prized stallion. The descendants of this horse became known to the people of Mexico as the horses of Palomino, or as *Ysabellas* in honor of the queen. According to legend, after Juan died all the golden horses were turned loose, and many years later found their way into the stables of wealthy ranchers in California. Because of their rich beauty, Palominos became prized possessions of these horse-loving people.

Other breeds such as the Morgan, Quarter Horse, Thoroughbred, Arabian and American Saddle Bred were brought to California to improve the conformation of the Palominos. This resulted in three fixed types of Palominos being developed: stock and Western show mounts from Quarter Horses; pleasure horses, jumpers and polo ponies from all strains; and flashy show and parade horses from Saddle Breds.

Palominos were classified as a color, not a breed, for the golden coats of Palomino parents are seldom passed on to their young. The color may come unexpectedly from any mating, no matter what the parent strains may be. Sometimes breeders can cross Palominos with horses of bright chestnut coloring and achieve the gold they are seeking.

There are two registries for Palominos, since golden horses can appear among other breeds, and can be entered into a registry for their breeding, as well as into a Palomino registry for color. These are then known as double-registered horses. Because Palominos come from many different families, they do not have a height or weight classification, except that they cannot be under 14 hands tall. They possess the qualities and traits of their breed association along with the flashy coloring.

Palominos' coats can vary in blond shades from light to dark, and their manes and tails must always be silvery-white or ivory. Many have white stockings and a white blaze on the face. Dark skin must appear beneath the gold, and their eyes should be dark hazel or brown. Palominos can have neither Pinto nor Appaloosa markings. Draft horses and ponies are forbidden in the Palomino registries, although the gold color does appear in these breeds.

The most widely known Palominos are the glamorous high-stepping parade mounts. The striking presence created by their glowing coats with sparkling manes and tails against costumes of fine silver saddlery and trappings can be seen in colorful parades throughout the world.

The Palomino is also popular at shows which feature classes for parade horses. They are judged on their parading manner, the rider posture and the quality of workmanship in the parade equipment. These adornments are of either silver or gold. Some are set with precious stones, including diamonds and rubies, and their prices run into the thousands of dollars. Substitutes for pure silver are barred from these classes at most large shows.

The parading Palominos are trained to perform showy artificial gaits, and they seem to sense their beauty as they strut ever so arrogantly under all their glittering finery.

THE LIPIZZAN

Over four centuries ago, beginning in the year 1565, the beautiful and aristocratic Lipizzans were created. They originated from Spanish horses of Arab and Barb ancestry, which were imported into Austria by Emperor Maximilian II. Their name was taken from the small town Lipizza near the Adriatic Sea.

The breed was used exclusively by the Hapsburgs, the royal family of Austria. No commoner was allowed to own one of these horses. Only nobles serving in the Hapsburg armies were given Lipizzan stallions to ride, and daring movements, to be used in war, were taught to these horses. These movements shielded the riders and terrified enemy foot soldiers during battle.

When the Lipizzans were no longer needed in warfare, horsemanship was improved and riding schools were formed. The most famous one is the Spanish Riding School of Vienna, so called because of the Lipizzans' Spanish origin.

In 1735, Austria's Emperor Charles VI considered the leaps and plunges of the Lipizzans so spectacular that he had a magnificent hall built for the Riding School. The ballroom in this hall, where even today the horses perform, was constructed so that spectators were provided with an unobstructed view of the horses rearing and dancing to the music of classical composers.

At the Spanish Riding School, the art of *haute ecole,* or advanced horsemanship, was formed according to the teachings of Xenophon, a Greek writer and horseman who lived in 400 B.C. This man believed that a horse could be more easily trained if achievements were praised and if mistakes were corrected in a gentle manner.

Only Lipizzan stallions are trained at the Spanish Riding School. Mares are used strictly for breeding purposes and never ridden. They are highly prized and considered most valuable. Colts stay with the mares until they are ready for the first stages of their lengthy schooling.

Unlike many breeds of horses who begin their training at a much earlier age, Lipizzans are not even saddled until they are five. Beginning at the age of four they first fulfill a year of intensive schooling without any rider. It takes nearly five years to perfect their movements, and usually the horses are teamed with the same instructor for the entire period.

Great patience and dedication on the part of the instructors show in the skills mastered by the Lipizzan stallions. Many of the complicated exercises taught at the school are taken directly from the movements used by the war horses. Today these exercises are performed specifically for beauty, and exemplify the highest level of *dressage,* which means to guide the horse through complex and rhythmic maneuvers with very slight signals from the rider. These signals are known as aids by equestrians, and are almost invisible.

The most advanced and difficult movements are called the *Airs Above the Ground,* and are achieved by those stallions with the greatest intelligence and strength. The *Airs* are made up of very specific maneuvers: the *Courbette,* when the horse does several jumps on the hind legs while holding the forelegs off the ground; the *Capriole,* where the horse leaps from all four feet, and at the highest point, kicks the hind legs violently rearward; the *Croupade,* which is a jump identical to the *Capriole* except the horse tucks the hind legs up under the body; the *Piaffe,* which is a cadenced trot executed in place, requiring extreme bending of the hindquarters; the *Pirouette,* which can be a stationary canter in a circling motion or a rearing movement where the horse executes a full turn on the hind legs; and the *Levade* (pictured), in which the horse squats on the hindquarters, lifts the forelegs off the ground, tucks them under the body and maintains a forty-five degree angle.

Lipizzans were originally many different colors. But they have been bred for white over the centuries and it is very rare that they are found in other colors. All Lipizzans, however, are born black or dark gray and become lighter as they get older, usually turning pure white between seven and ten years of age. Lipizzans possess elegance and grace along with their great strength and dignity. They are perhaps one of the rarest breeds in existence today.

Often seen on tour throughout the world, these horses leave audiences breathless, for they seem to be doing the impossible. The performances of the dazzling white Lipizzans, presenting themselves with poise and discipline, are wondrous exhibitions of courage and love, for the stallions obviously take great pride and joy in their accomplishments.

THE DRAFT HORSE

The draft horse breeds are chiefly used to haul heavy loads. They were of great importance on farms and in cities a few decades ago, before the arrival of heavy farm machinery, automobiles and trucks. Teams of work horses still plow the fields of rural areas in parts of the world. But most commonly draft horses appear at county fairs in weight-pulling matches, in parade hitches of six or eight, pulling large brewery wagons or heavy ornate circus wagons, and at large horse shows in halter classes.

Some modern draft breeds are believed to be descended from the huge war horses of medieval Europe — the type that carried knights in armor, weapons, heavy saddles and bulky horse armor, totalling over 400 pounds.

Cold-bloods, as draft horses are called, are known for their gentle disposition and their willingness to work. All of them have enormous, well-muscled bodies, and possess superior strength. Some weigh well over a ton and reach heights of more than 17 hands.

The Belgian is perhaps the strongest of the draft horses. This breed holds the record for pulling weight in contests. They work in pairs, moving 4000 pounds or more. Belgians originated in the fertile lowlands of Belgium. It is believed they gained their great pulling power from many years of tilling the heavy soil of that country. The Belgian's color can be roan, bay, chestnut or sorrel with a flaxen mane and tail. They are best known for their immense size, strength and good disposition.

The Shire is the largest and tallest of the draft horses. Their long legs and neck create a noble look, and they move with a proud carriage. They have amazing strength, and a pair of Shires can pull weights of up to several tons. This breed retains the heavy feathery hair on the lower legs and fetlocks that protected them from the razor-sharp grass of their native homeland — Cambridgeshire and Lincolnshire in England. This horse is found in bay, brown, sorrel or black with white markings.

The Clydesdale is the national horse of Scotland, where the breed originated in the valley of the river Clyde. There in the moist soil they developed the exceptionally strong, healthy legs and feet for which they are noted. Clydesdales are not as heavy as other draft horses. This handsome breed possesses a high and springy leg action, which produces a showy prancing appearance. Hitches of Clydesdales pulling heavy and decorative wagons can be seen in parades. Their popular color is bay with large areas of white on the face and legs.

The Percheron was developed by farmers in La Perche, a district of France. They were first used as work horses and coach horses. They are powerfully built, yet trimmer than the other draft breeds, with less leg hair and smaller feet. It is thought they may have some Arab blood, for in spite of their size, they seem unusually active with a very stylish gait. Percherons are reliable, calm and have a steady disposition. These traits plus their ability to hold a slow, even canter, and their broad backs make them the choice of bareback acrobats. In the circus these horses are called rosinbacks, because their backs are dusted with rosin to insure good footing for the performers. Percherons nearly always appear in dapple-gray, white or black.

The Suffolk Punch originated in Suffolk County in Eastern England and is believed to be the oldest of the draft breeds. Bred to plow the fields of their fertile homeland, the Suffolk developed strong stocky legs, a short thick neck and powerful hindquarters. They are called the Suffolk Punch because their massive bodies look rotund and "punchy." They have less hair than other draft breeds and the sleekness of their coats gives them a just-groomed appearance. Suffolks have become famous for their docility and kindness, their willingness to serve, their endurance, strength and longevity — they are often still working in their twenties. They are always colored chestnut, with a slightly lighter mane and tail. A white star is sometimes found on the forehead.

THE PONY –
SHETLAND and WELSH

Ponies make ideal mounts for young riders since they are better proportioned for the child than a large horse. Not so easily frightened, ponies are frequently more intelligent as well. Because of their calm disposition, ponies will tolerate the constant attention given by their young masters. Naturally hardy and rugged, ponies require a minimum of shelter and simple rations at all times of the year. Two of the most popular pony breeds with children are the Shetland and the Welsh.

Shetlands are widely distributed, and perhaps are the most affectionate of all ponies. They are the smallest of the breeds and, for their size, the strongest of any horse.

Originating in the raw and wintry Shetland Islands, far north of Scotland, these diminutive horses are believed to have evolved from ancient Icelandic or Celtic ponies. The island terrain was rough and barren with poor soil and constant bitter winds from the sea. These severe subarctic conditions resulted in the ponies becoming smaller, tougher and extremely sure-footed.

In the islands, Shetlands were used for carrying loads of peat and seaweed. They helped plow the rocky earth, and were used for transportation by children and grownups alike. Later, Shetlands pulled coal carts in the mines of Northern England. They were called pit ponies, and some of them never saw daylight.

Around 1900, many of these small horses, known as Shelties in England, were imported into the United States. Through careful breeding, a more suitable riding pony for children was developed.

Shetlands are divided into two classifications: the English type and the American type. Because of their blocky bodies, the English type do not make good animals for riding, but they are very appropriate cart ponies. Shetlands of the American variety are taller and slighter built, and more active with better gaits. Not only are they ridden by children, but are shown in horse shows at halter and in harness classes by both young people and adults. Shetlands make good jumpers, and can sometimes clear a three-foot fence. Shetlands are often seen in four to eight pony hitches, pulling small wagons in parades.

Some breeds are measured in inches rather than hands as in the case of large horses. The average height of the American Shetland is usually 42 inches, with a maximum of 46 inches. The English type stands 40 inches, with a 42-inch maximum.

Noted for a lifespan of thirty years or better, Shetlands are especially good-natured and lovable, with neat small heads and large kind eyes. In the British Isles, these ponies are usually black, brown or bay. The American variety, however, can be silver-dapple, black, bay, brown, chestnut, roan, gray, white, or spotted like a pinto. Their coats are thick and woolly in the winter, becoming sleek in the summer — but Shetlands always display an abundant mane, forelock and tail.

The origin of the Welsh pony is vague. They are believed to be descended from the small tough horses left to run wild in Great Britain after the Roman occupation in the fourth and fifth centuries. Desert horses of Arab and Barb ancestry somehow crossed with these horses which led a semi-wild existence, roaming the rough terrain and fending for themselves. They survived on sparse vegetation in a land where winters were miserably cold. Because of their hard and rugged life, these horses decreased to pony size but grew stronger, healthier and more intelligent. Locating in the remote Welsh Mountains of Northern Wales, they became the Welsh pony, also called the Welsh Mountain pony.

The apparent Arab-Barb ancestry has contributed to the Welsh pony's traits. Their heads appear fine and shapely with small tapering muzzles. The face is dished with wide-set and expressive eyes and small, pointed ears. Their slender and graceful neck is set well into deep sloping shoulders and a wide chest. Well-muscled with a short strong back and exceptionally sound legs and feet, Welsh ponies have a lofty carriage and — in action — display a high-flung tail.

Welsh ponies come in two sizes: one stands under 12:2 hands and the other can measure up to 14 hands. The larger size can easily carry the weight of an adult rider. The coloring may be white, black, bay, brown, chestnut, gray, dun, or cream, but never spotted. Blazes and white stockings are common.

Welsh ponies are remarkable jumpers, sometimes negotiating obstacles over four and one-half feet high in the show-ring and in the hunt field. Possessed with swiftness, agility and stamina, these ponies are noted for their companionable nature. Though gentle and docile, they are spirited, making excellent mounts for more advanced young riders who wish to show and jump.

IMAGINATIVE
COLOR & STORY ALBUMS
FROM TROUBADOR PRESS

Airplanes	Exotic Animals
All About Horses	Giants & Goblins
Ballet	The Great Whales
Cats & Kittens	Mythical Monsters
Cowboys	North American Indians
Dinosaurs	Northwest Coast Indians
Dolls	Trains
Egyptian Gods	Tropical Fish
Enchanted Kingdom	Unicorns
Wonderful World of Horses	

Also look for our Troubador Funbooks and
Troubador Color-and-Find Hidden Pictures.

Troubador Press books are available wherever books are sold or can be ordered directly from the publisher.
Customer Service Department, 390 Murray Hill Parkway, East Rutherford, NJ 07073

TROUBADOR PRESS
an imprint of
PSS!
PRICE STERN SLOAN